Conflicts, Machines, Beliefs, and Decisions

il

Philosophische Hefte

Band 9

Herausgegeben von

Prof. Dr. Axel Gelfert
Prof. Dr. Thomas Gil

Conflicts, Machines, Beliefs, and Decisions

Thomas Gil

Logos Verlag Berlin

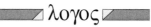 λογος

Philosophische Hefte

Herausgegeben von

Prof. Dr. Axel Gelfert
Prof. Dr. Thomas Gil
Institut für Philosophie, Literatur-, Wissenschafts- und
Technikgeschichte
Technische Universität Berlin

Bibliografische Information der Deutschen
Nationalbibliothek

Die Deutsche Nationalbibliothek verzeichnet diese
Publikation in der Deutschen Nationalbibliografie;
detaillierte bibliografische Daten sind im Internet über
http://dnb.d-nb.de abrufbar.

ISBN 978-3-8325-4974-9
ISSN 2567-1758

Logos Verlag Berlin GmbH
Comeniushof, Gubener Str. 47,
10243 Berlin

Tel.:   +49 (0)30 / 42 85 10 90
Fax: +49 (0)30 / 42 85 10 92

http://www.logos-verlag.de

Contents

Preface

"Intelligent Machines" and brilliant technologies are changing radically our practical reality, that is, the reality in which we act and interact with other people, believing and deciding, agreeing and disagreeing, and always entangled in never ending conflicts. The following essays describe and analyse all these components of our practical world. They are about what it is to believe something, how we make up our minds and decide, what it means that conflicts and disagreements are not eliminable, and the fact that new technological developments are substantially changing the way we live.

Conflicts, Disagreements, and Debates

Conflicts characterize the social world in which individual human beings coexist, act and react, cooperating sometimes, fighting most of the time. Conflicts pervade social life: epistemic and practical conflicts. Desires, preferences, interests, emotions, goals, intentions and plans are the most important items that give rise to practical conflicts. And those same items combined with experiences, degrees of evidence, information levels and testimonies are the sources of epistemic disagreements, disputes and debates.

Believing, acting and deciding in the social world, we experience most of the time conflicts, disagreements and controversies.

Conflicts may be epistemic or practical. Sometimes, they are latent, and not expressed or understood in explicit terms. Disagreements are mainly epistemic. They concern beliefs and opinions. Frequently, they can be expressed in precise sentences and statements. Disputes or controversies are conceived of in this essay as academic or intellectual enterprises serving to facilitate the confrontation of different and divergent standpoints, views or positions.

1 Conflicts

In order to explain what conflicts are, I adopt the theoretical perspective of a "situational approach" according to which conflicts are not mental entities existing in an ideal realm (a domain of ideal objects) but "existential" or practical situations in which acting and interacting individuals are involved, pulled in different (not compatible or divergent) directions, and incapable of finding ways of proceeding, acceptable (or favourable) to all involved agents. Thus seen, conflicts are dynamic, relational and "existential" (in J. Dewey's sense of this term).

Conflicts are "dynamic". They are factors that cause changes in the situations in which they come about and develop. They have phases and tendencies. They create tensions, pressures, and strains.

Conflicts are "situational" then they need certain constellations to come about and to exist. They presuppose elements or components of such constellations, related in specific ways.

Conflicts are "existential", that is, they are relevant for the individuals and groups involved. They require appropriate coping behaviour, and adequate solutions.

For the first generation of American sociologists, who were mainly reformists and shared a "melioristic" approach to social questions, conflicts were something positive as they were seen as performing decidedly positive functions

Those founding fathers of social theory knew that conflicts can tear apart individuals, groups and societies. But they decided to concentrate on their positive functions of maintaining group boundaries and preventing the withdrawal of members from a group. For them, conflicts accomplish group-binding functions (increasing internal cohesion), facilitate the establishment and maintenance of balances of power, and create associations and coalitions.

There are different kinds of sources and causes of conflicts: divergent desires and preferences, opposite emotions, interests and goals, intentions and plans that are not compatible, struggles over values and claims to status, power and resources, and many things more.

There are two main types of conflicts: theoretical or epistemic conflicts, and practical (moral, political, economic and social) conflicts.

I would use the concept "conflict" only to refer to the so-called practical conflicts, that is, conflicts that affect agents and deciders, and, in the case of theoretical and epistemic conflicts, I would propose to use the concept of disagreement instead of keeping on speaking about conflicts.

2 Disagreements

Disagreement seems to be everywhere. People disagree continually. Disagreements can concern just about anything. They can arise from politics, religion, ethics, sports, history, science, business, entertainment, and of course philosophy. Disagreements are omnipresent, in public and in personal life. They concern mainly two different sorts of questions: how to act, and what to believe.

In our private lives we disagree with our parents, our spouses and partners, our friends and colleagues. In the public sphere, politicians disagree about how to spend enormous amounts of money, or about what laws to pass. Philosophically, we disagree when we discuss matters like free will, time travel, God's existence, capital punishment, morality, scientific theories, justice and distributive policies.

In daily life and in the sciences (in physical, mental, and moral science), we disagree about facts, and about values. For instance, we might disagree over "Shakespeare was left-handed" as well as over value questions as "The capital punishment system is immoral" or "Abortion is immoral".

Especially important are the disagreements over facts that have a large bearing on our lives. Disputes over factual claims may be relevant too when it comes to value judgements. So, for instance, when we examine the question whether "advanced interrogation techniques" amount to "torture", and then ask whether "torture" is unethical in every circumstance.

In general terms, our disagreements are over beliefs and actions. Belief-disagreements are over the truth of a claim. Action-disagreements are about what to do (or omit doing). When it comes to belief-disagreement, there are three options with respect to a certain claim: believe it, disbelieve it, or suspend judgement on it. When it comes to action-disagreement, there are just two options with respect to an action x: do x, don't do x.

Despite the distinction between disagreements over what to believe and what to do, we can achieve simplicity and uniformity in the disagreement-talk by construing disagreements over what to do as disagreements over what to believe. The way to do it would be to say that if we disagree over whether to do action x, we disagree over the truth of the claim "We should do x" or "x is the best thing for us to do". Following such a translation of action-disagreements into claim-disagreements, we can easily construe all disagreements as disagreements about what to believe where the belief may or may not concern an action.

Belief-disagreements may be about easy or harder questions.

It is well possible that two reasonable people can come to different yet reasonable (in the sense of not stupid) answers to a single question when they have the same data, including the same background knowledge, having more or less the same cognitive ability, and having worked on the question for a comparable amount of time. The question about which they disagree may be an easy question or a hard question. Easy questions are easy because the disagreement can be easily resolved according to pertinent procedures and depending on the kind of question. Not so the hard questions for which there is not a trustworthy informational basis, or whose resolution presupposes sharing certain premises, perspectives and views.

When we realize that we disagree with someone over a certain claim, we can react to that realization in a rational way: we can start a debate in order to find out whether we should retain our belief, suspend judgement, or adopt the other view.

3 Debates

A debate is a "verbal", "social", and "rational" activity aimed at convincing a critic or disputant of the acceptability of a standpoint by putting forward a set of propositions justifying or refuting the central proposition expressed in the standpoint. The main proponents of the so-called "Pragma-Dialectical Approach" to the theory of argumentation define in such (or similar) terms the concept of a debate. They speak about argumentations. But they mean "debates". And they are right because debates are linguistic performances, goal-directed, and addressing other agents who may or may not share our beliefs, convictions or standpoints.

In certain societies and cultural contexts debates are conceived of as fights with winners and losers. In other cultural contexts, in more reconciliatory milieus, debates are seen as pleasant conversations presenting different options, and inviting us to come together in an open thinking process.

Debates and arguments are one of the paradigmatic examples used by George Lakoff and Mark Johnson to show how we, thinking, tend most of the time to understand one kind of thing in terms of another. In our Western culture, so their argument, we tend to understand debates as "wars" where there are winners and losers, attacking and defending strategies, gaining and losing of ground. Other cultures could be imagined according to Lakoff and Johnson where debates and arguments are viewed as dances, the participants as performers, and the goal as a performance in a balanced and aesthetically pleasing way (Lakoff, Johnson, 4f.).

Understanding debates as "games of strategy" may be, however, advantageous. "Game theory" is a well developed branch of behavioural science providing many useful models to better understand and explain human behaviour in situations in which various and divergent interests, motives, informational levels, and alternatives are involved. Game theory provides, in other words, intellectual tools for the analysis of conflict situations, and debates come about where there are conflicts of opinions and standpoints. In debates, opponents direct arguments at each other with the aim of convincing the opponent and making him or her see things in a specific way.

Debates can be won or lost. There are indeed better and worse arguments for the debated issues, questions, views and standpoints. But debates are not only about the logical strength of arguments. Many other non-logical factors play a role in debates: factors not to be neglected that strategic game theory takes into account.

Debates are not resolvable by rational procedures alone. As they result from a clash of existentially relevant incompatible or partly incompatible views and standpoints, debates are about persistent views, images, positions, perspectives, and are efforts to induce opponents to change their point of view. No easy task indeed. Anatol Rapoport proposed three different ways or methods to get to a resolution: the "Pavlovian", the "Freudian", and the "Rogerian" path (Rapoport, 273). Translated into a more adequate terminology, the first path would be a "behaviouristic" one, the second a "critical" way, the third way a "persuasive" one.

The "persuasive" way to resolution would concentrate not only on the logical strength of arguments but would insist on the motivational reasons debating individuals would have to change their views and convictions. While the first method, the "behaviouristic" way, forces and reinforces , sanctions positively and negatively, and is strictly directive, the second method, the "critical " way, reveals and makes manifest problematic underpinnings and presuppositions of the held views and convictions. Only the third way is "permissive" and "non-directive". It offers alternative ways of seeing things, and it shows the positive effects of choosing them. Without ignoring the plausibility (and limited validity) of adopted positions and standpoints, it shows possible paths to leave behind dilemmatic and aporetic situations.

The third "permissive" and "non-directive" way is supposed to be collectively chosen by all the involved debating actors experiencing in a learning process what it means to transcend unnecessary limitations.

4 Bibliography

Coser, L., The Functions of Social Conflict (London: The Free Press of Glencoe, 1964).

Eemeren, F. H. van, Grootendorst, R., A Systematic Theory of Argumentation. The pragma-dialectical approach (Cambridge: Cambridge University Press, 2004)-

Frances, B., Disagreement (Cambridge: Polity Press, 2014).

Lakoff, G., Johnson, M., Metaphors We Live By (Chicago: The University of Chicago Press, 1981).

Rapoport, A., Fights, Games, and Debates (Michigan: The University of Michigan Press, 1960).

Rogers, C. R., Client-Centered Therapy (Boston: Houghton Mifflin Co., 1951).

Intelligent Machines

1 Artificial Intelligence

All living organisms are intelligent in different ways. They act and react adapting to their environments. They accomplish different functions that allow them to survive, better or worse.

Human beings, human organisms, are considered to be the most intelligent organisms as they are able to develop a complex mental life. Perceiving, experiencing, feeling, intending, willing, wishing and thinking, human organisms adapt to their environment, and manipulate objects and things that make it up. Like that, they transform substantially their environment creating new and artificial worlds.

Perceiving, feeling, wishing, willing, intending and thinking are intelligent mental functions characteristic of human beings.

Most people associate "intelligence" with the thinking capability. Thinking, we represent the world, we identify objects, and we say something about them, describing how they are and how they function. Thinking, we operate with ideas and concepts that refer to objects, and we utter propositions or statements about how the world is, and how it works, putting ideas and concepts together. Thinking, we infer propositions from propositions when we reason about what we already know.

Thomas Hobbes called this reasoning by which we get new propositions from old propositions "ratiocination". And he conceived of it as "computation". For Hobbes, to think is to "compute", that is, to count and to calculate. "Counting" is a mental operation that uses symbols and proceeds according to certain rules. As symbolic operation, counting is independent of any particular medium. It operates with symbols that are "produced", "identified" and "re-identified". Counting operations need always a medium in which they are embedded. But they are independent of the medium in the sense that they can be materialized in any number of different media.

That is actually the reason why counting operations can be accomplished by human beings and (calculating) machines and computers. Thus seen, there is nothing mysterious about counting, computing, and thinking. Mindless mechanisms could carry out counting operations, provided every single move is fully determined by a way of proceeding called "algorithm". "Algorithms" are infallible, step-by-step recipes for obtaining specific results. "Infallible" means the procedure is guaranteed to succeed in a finite number of steps, of course, assuming each step is carried out correctly. Proceeding "step-by-step" means three things: 1) the recipe prescribes one step at a time, i.e. one after another; 2) there are no options or uncertainties: after each step the next step is fully determined; 3) no ingenuity or insight is required, i.e. after each step the next step is obvious. Algorithms are therefore mindless prescriptions or routines that (sooner or later) always work. They are a straight schedule of instructions: do "A" first, then do "B" ... and finally do "Z".

That is the simple and basic beginning. Full-fledged Artificial Intelligence would be much more if it is supposed to catch up with what brains can do. Computers, robots, and other artificial agents will be able, without any doubt, to accomplish several brain (or mind) functions. That is after all the aim of Artificial Intelligence, namely, to develop and implement diverse information-processing capacities as human brains do. Therefore we see AI's practical applications already everywhere: in the home, the car, the office, the bank, the hospital, the Internet (including the Internet of Things) etc.

AI-devices and AI-techniques are of course intelligent because they can accomplish and achieve many things intelligent human beings can accomplish. But they are not natural intelligent human beings who feel and suffer, fall in love and experience pain, try to find meanings in their lives, and are deceived and enjoy what they are doing.

A truly intelligent system would certainly possess "functional consciousness". It would focus on or pay attention to different things at different times. A "human-level system" would be able to deliberate, and self-reflect. It would generate creative ideas, and even evaluate and assess them. But it would never have what some authors have called "phenomenal consciousness". It would discriminate as living human beings do. But it would have no "qualia" or subjective feelings concerning "what it is like" to do this or that, or to experience this or that. In order to have a "phenomenal consciousness" they would need more than algorithms and material stuff. They would need perhaps human stuff: human interaction with other human beings, body and community experiences, and all the things a "mortal" human life is made of.

2 Big Data

Collections, storage and analysis of data have been in every human society important activities. However, in the so-called "advanced information societies" data is fundamental.

In such societies large amounts of data in the form of images, videos, tweets, identity details, and all sorts of documents are being created at a rate unimaginable only a few decades ago. New data analysis techniques transform this data into useful information.

The increasingly vast amounts of structured, unstructured, and semi-structured data being generated minute by minute have contributed to what is named a "data explosion", and to the coming about of the digital age. Supermarkets, airlines, banks collect data on what we buy, about our travel arrangements, and our financial transactions, that is, data that can be used in commerce and medicine, and from which useful information can be extracted.

The development of computer technology made possible the collection, storage, and analysis of those amounts of data which due to their volume, variety, and velocity (the famous three "V"s) became "Big Data".

"Data is the new oil" is a catchy phrase to refer to this new development in industry, commerce and politics in the digital age. The phrase suggests that data (especially "big data") is extremely valuable but must, like oil, first be processed before that value can be realized.

Data to become valuable information must be grouped, classified, related, that means, analysed and properly administered. With "big data" a paradigmatic change has taken place. For small data analysis, procedures were well-established and human intervention was necessary: someone came up with an idea, formulating a hypothesis or model, and devising ways to test its predictions. Working with big data we do not follow these procedures any more. Now machines, intelligent machines, not scientists, are predominant. Machines are now the agents that find correlations in data. Machines provide now means of prediction based on the strength of the relationships between variables. And they do this in all imaginable sectors: in medicine, in business, in politics.

In data-driven "worlds", robotic and all sorts of smart devices will be the protagonists, increasingly taken the place of people, and persistently determining the ways to do things.

Big data is power. It makes an impact in all areas, and it affects everyone. Its potential for good is enormous. Its abuse will be difficult to prevent.

3 Digital Worlds

The title "Digital Worlds" refers to the fact that digitization is becoming universal, that is, that there is no sphere, realm, doing or activity in the digital age that cannot be affected by a progressive process of digitization.

Autonomous vehicles, from cars to planes, seem almost inevitable. Planes can already fly themselves, including taking off and landing. Drones are currently used in farming for intelligent crop-spraying and also for military purposes. Commercial drone delivery services using GPS is a growing branch. And of course "smart" and "autonomous" cars are being developed. However, the potential for cyber-attacks on them will need to be addressed before the technology becomes fully public. Also possible malfunctions that could cause injury or death to humans as well as considerable damage to material objects need to be addressed.

"Smart homes" on the basis of the "Internet of Things", that is, on the basis of a vast number of electronic sensors connected to the Internet are becoming ever more a daily reality. Electrical appliances such as washing machines, refrigerators, and home-cleaning robots are part of the smart home and managed remotely through smartphones, laptops, or home speakers. Since all these systems are Internet controlled they are potentially at risk from hackers.

The "Internet of Things" and "Big Data" management techniques, working together, are the key to "smart cities" with driverless cars, remote health monitoring, smart homes, tele-commuting and smart energy systems. In such smart cities there will be a huge array of radio-frequency identification (RFID) taps and wireless sensors, sending data from individual devices to a central location for analysis and facilitating like that among other things street lighting regulation, traffic monitoring, and even garbage tracking.

In such digital worlds data security would be of paramount importance.

4 Mortal Beings

Digitization is becoming omnipresent. Traditional actions and transactions, ways of doing things and activities are being "digitally" transformed, that is, they are becoming ever more "data-based" and "data-guided". Computers are not only tools for commercial enterprises to improve efficiency, cut costs, and generate profits. Ever-smaller and ever-smarter machines have changed nature and dynamics of commerce. Massive amounts of collected unstructured data allow enterprises to predict what customers want to buy based on previous sales and transactions or website activity. Vast amounts of collected data including addresses, payment information, and details of everything individuals have ever looked at or actually bought are used to construct customer profiles allowing similar individuals and their recommendations to be matched.

The world of healthcare is also being changed substantially. Medical diagnosis, epidemic prediction, gauging the public response to official health warnings, and the reduction of costs associated with health care systems are being systematically digitized.

Patient records are stored. Big data is collected, stored, and analysed to provide improved patient care and reduce cost. Unpleasant reactions to medication are monitored. Online medical advice proliferates. Via wearable devices, the number of steps individuals take each day, caloric requirements, sleep patterns, heart rate and blood pressure, among many other things, are counted, measured, tracked, and stored, generating a veritable cascade of data that provide health care professionals with valuable information as a means for recognizing changes and helping avoid all sorts of health risks.

Evidently, data security becomes then a significant challenge. Big data allows to predict the spread of disease, and to personalize medicine. But how is the privacy of the individual's medical data to be protected? Questions arise then as to who owns the data, where it is being stored, who can access and use it, and how secure it is from cyber-attacks. Ethical and legal issues are abundant concerning all these questions and challenges.

"Artificial Intelligence", "Big Data", "Internet of Things", and many other similar catchy formulae are symbolic terms used to refer to a new "digital age" that is coming about, that is, to a new social, technological, and economic revolution brought about by brilliant and intelligent technologies: a "Second Machine Age" (to use E. Brynjolfsson's and A. McAfee's expression). In such an age, potentially everything is getting digitized so that our working and living conditions will change radically. Digitization means simply the operation of encoding all kinds of information as a stream of bits (the language of computers and their kins).

Much money is involved, and many interested agents and prophets proclaim new eras always trying to manipulate the way we think about the new transformations. Certainly, many problems we are confronted with will be solved. But new challenges and difficulties will come about that may transcend our powers and abilities to cope with what is new. After all, we as individuals are only contingent, "mortal" beings.

5 Bibliography

Boden, M. A., Artificial Intelligence. A Very Short Introduction (Oxford: Oxford University Press, 2018).

Brynjolfsson, E., McAffee, A., The Second Machine Age. Work, Progress, and Prosperity in a Time of Brilliant Technologies (New York: W. W. Norton & Company, 2014).

Holmes, D. E., Big Data. A Very Short Introduction (Oxford: Oxford University Press, 2017).

Believing

Living in the world, we get and process information about our environment. We open our eyes and see things that happen. We hear stories about what happened in the past. We touch stuffs and materials of different sizes, shapes and consistencies. We smell pleasant and unpleasant odours. And we eat tasty food avoiding eating what does not taste to us.

On the basis of acquired information, we form beliefs, assumptions, conjectures and hypotheses about what the world is made of, that is, what there is and how it functions. Further experience will confirm or disconfirm our beliefs, conjectures and hypotheses, causing us to give them up or allowing us to hold on to them.

This operation of forming beliefs and conjectures about the world is performed in everyday life and in science. The informational basis in daily life and in scientific contexts may be different. The mechanism, however, is the same.

Karl P. Popper described the method of falsification, that is, the method of testing and trying to refute conjectures and hypotheses as the method of science. In daily life, we are not primarily interested in falsifying whatever we may have assumed, but in moving around in the world and coping with all the challenges we are confronted with. In daily life like in science, however, we keep on guessing about the world forming conjectures and hypotheses, and trying to predict what is going to be the case in the future on the basis of what we presently believe according to our acquired experiential evidence.

1 Believing Something

H. H. Price distinguishes in "Some Considerations about Belief" two elements in belief: 1) the entertaining of a proposition, 2) the assenting to or adopting of that proposition (Price, in: Griffiths, 43). The first element, the entertainment of a proposition, is not only contained in the mental operations of believing and disbelieving but also in doubting, questioning, supposing, etc. Entertaining a proposition means simply thinking of something as such and such without assenting necessarily to it. The second element, the element of assenting or adopting the entertained proposition, has an emotional side to it, as we feel a feeling of sureness or confidence when we believe something. It is obvious that any belief may be mistaken. However much evidence we have for a proposition, and however confident we feel about it, it may still be false (this being, indeed, part of the definition of belief).

Believing (for some authors) seems to be the relation in which a proposition stands to a mind cognizing it, or the cognitive relation in which the believer stands to a certain proposition. Other authors prefer to understand belief as a conjunction of two elements: 1) the entertained proposition, and 2) a disposition to act as if the proposition were true. Frank Ramsey sketched a theory based on the assumption that "disposition to action" is a general criterion for belief, by which degrees of belief can be measured by a sort of generalized betting. And he propounded this as a theory of probability.

The constraints beliefs impose upon us are not always action-related or behavioural. Believing something is: believing something as true, so that everything that we believe is believed "sub specie veri". Such a constraint is in very many and most typical cases "dispositional", but not necessarily in all cases.

Beliefs may have several functions. They may help us make predictions and select actions. Some beliefs help us understand a subject in more detail. Others inspire creativity. Some generate emotions. Others make us feel good or buttress confidence.

We get our beliefs from our senses (by seeing, hearing, and touching), by explaining things, or deriving consequences of what we already believe.

Beliefs come always with other beliefs, in networks or webs of beliefs. And we evaluate them in complex ways considering evidence for and against them.

We hold some beliefs more strongly than others, and we are able to describe degrees of belief (or belief strengths) using sentences like "Definite, it is so", "It is quite likely to be so", "It is possible that", "It is doubtful that", etc.

2 Not Anything

What we believe has something to do with the persons we are, the places we have been to, the times we have experienced, the local communities we belong to.

Beliefs have always objects and contents. Objects of beliefs may be things (particular things) or classes of things, properties or states of affairs, non-existent things, the way things could have been but are not, or the way things are and must be, etc. Most beliefs have propositional contents: we believe that something is such and such, or that something is the case. Some beliefs are related to others merely associatively, while other beliefs are related or connected to other beliefs inferentially.

Beliefs as opposed to perceptions may be stimulus-independent, that is, they may be about objects that are not present. Perception involves always a form of "stimulus-dependent" contact with the world. Indeed, we can have beliefs about things that are imperceptible in principle. Whereas perception provides us with access to only a small range of objects, the reach of beliefs is (theoretically) unlimited. However, all our beliefs are connected to certain conditions that have something to do with the particular contexts in which our believing activity is situated and singular features of our environment that are more salient or significant to us than other features and aspects. Therefore, there is a variation in the contents of our beliefs, that is, there is a variation in the contents of our ontological, religious, moral and political beliefs. The variation may concern the generality and abstractness (versus particularity and concreteness) of our beliefs. It may also concern whether those beliefs are more holistic or more atomistic. And, of course, the variation is an effect of the range of beliefs that are practically accessible to the believers, so that, even if the basic cognitive capacities of human beings do not fundamentally vary, the single beliefs that are readily available to the members of certain groups, communities and certain societies may differ in radical ways from those that are available to the members of other groups, communities and societies.

3 Refutations

Refutations are easily to be had. If I believe that swans, that is, all swans are white and run into or encounter a black swan, the propositional content of my belief has been objectively refuted even if I may be unwilling to give up my belief. My belief (or better: the propositional content of my belief) is incompatible then with real facts of the world. And the rational way of proceeding would be to stop believing what I had believed. Refutations force us to give up or modify and refine our beliefs.

K. R. Popper made "refutability" (or "testability" and "falsifiability") the criterion of scientific theories. For Popper, good scientific theories make risky predictions and are therefore refutable when confronted with reality. Good scientific theories "forbid" certain things to happen. The more a theory forbids, therefore, the better it is so that a theory which is not refutable by any conceivable event is non-scientific. Irrefutability is for Popper not a virtue of a theory as some people may think but a vice. "Refutability" became thus in Popper's philosophy of science the "criterion of demarcation" between scientific and non-scientific theories.

Popper thought as Hume did that it is not possible to infer a theory from observation statements. But he thought that we can, after having come somehow to any theory, test it or try to refute it by observation statements. Attempted refutations became in such a way fundamental for Popper's theory of science. Repeated observations and experiments are the tests of theoretical conjectures and hypotheses, i.e. of theories as conjectures and hypotheses.

4 Webs of Beliefs

It is not possible to have just one belief. Believing something means always having several interrelated or interconnected beliefs. Individual beliefs exist always in webs of beliefs, related and connected to other beliefs. In such webs, our beliefs support partially one another by partially explaining one another. And it is in the light of the full body of our beliefs (or at least of some sub-set of such "body") that new beliefs gain acceptance or rejection, so that any independent merits of a specific belief tend to be less decisive. Beliefs rest most of the time on further beliefs. And if we want to get a belief of ours to be accepted by someone else, the question of support is doubled: we have to consider first what support sufficed for it in our case and then how much of the same support is ready for it in the new setting.

In "Mental Events", Donald Davidson speaks about the "holism" that characterizes mental phenomena like believing, intending, desiring, hoping, knowing, perceiving, noticing, remembering, and so on. Assuming and assigning beliefs cannot therefore be an atomistic enterprise. Davidson writes: "There is no assigning beliefs to a person one by one on the basis of his verbal behaviour, his choices, or other local signs no matter how plain and evident, for we make sense of particular beliefs only as they cohere with other beliefs, with preferences, with intentions, hopes, fears, expectations, and the rest ... the content of a propositional attitude derives from its place in the pattern" (Davidson, 1989, 221).

Beliefs, like propositions, have logical relations. The identity of a belief cannot be separated from its place in the logical network of other beliefs and it cannot be relocated in the network without being somehow transformed. This is so because of the "holism of the mental". In Davidson's own words: "This is the holism of the mental, the interdependence of various aspects of mentality" (Davidson, 2001, 123f.). We simply cannot believe something without believing many other things.

5 Scientific Beliefs

Scientific beliefs, like ordinary beliefs, are always related and connected to other beliefs in webs and networks that may be called theoretical frameworks or theories. Some of them may be complex beliefs or higher order beliefs as they are not about objects but about other beliefs.

Theories or theoretical networks in which scientific beliefs exist provide coherence and consistency, compatibility and logical dependence. Such frameworks contain not only beliefs but also "disbeliefs", disbeliefs being a case of belief. Theoretical frameworks are sometimes characterized by their "nonbeliefs", that is, by their specific absence of opinion or their specific suspended judgements. Theories may simply ignore and neglect certain sentences. They then neither believe them true nor believe them false.

Scientific theories are systems of beliefs. They organize the relations and interactions of a set of beliefs so that certain expectations are supported, and others not. If some expected event does not occur, the problem of selecting certain interlocking beliefs for revision comes up. This is what happens when an experiment is made to check a scientific theory and the result is not what the theory predicted. The theory is then to be revised somehow. When single observations show that a theoretical system of beliefs must be overhauled, there is always the possibility of choosing which of those interlocking beliefs to revise.

Beliefs, in ordinary life and in science, face the tribunal of observation "not singly but in a body"

(Quine, Ullian, 13). Failure of existing beliefs and their organization is the prelude to a search for new beliefs or a new organization.

In science, we may call our beliefs hypotheses. Calling a belief a hypothesis says nothing as what the belief is about, how firmly it is held, or how well founded it is. Calling it a hypothesis suggests rather what sort of reason we have for adopting or entertaining it.

A scientific theory would be a system of hypotheses that can accommodate all observations to date in a specific field of research. But not all hypotheses contained in a specific theoretical framework have the same status. There are, indeed, different kinds of hypotheses in scientific theories. Some are considered to be "self-evident", others are seen as "common knowledge" (though not self-evident), others are vouched for by authority in varying degrees, and others have simply worked all right so far.

6 Hypothetical Thinking

In ordinary life and in the sciences we rationally expect certain things to happen. So, to take an example given by Quine and Ullian, we expect toothpaste to exude when we squeeze the tube. Scientists could cite general principles about what happens to liquids or soft solids under pressure. Ordinary people would more likely support their expectation in terms of their past experience with tubes and their squeezing. What happens in such simple doings is related to general hypotheses or laws only in ways which normally remain far in the background. Were the activity not to succeed on a given squeezing we would surely not want to rewrite our physics. We consider such hypotheses as that the toothpaste in the tube had been used up, that it was blocked by some foreign object, or that it hardened. We would thus explain the failure of our expectation in the least sweeping terms available, making the revision in our belief web as small as possible.

The method of framing general hypotheses, by generalizing from observed cases to all cases of the kind, is called induction. Induction is the expectation that similar things will behave similarly. Induction is not a procedure alternative to hypothesis. It is a case of hypothesis or hypothetical thinking.

"Hypothesis" where successful is a two-way street. It extends back to explain the past, and it extends forward to predict the future. There are five qualities (Quine would say "virtues") that characterize good hypotheses. Good hypotheses are "conservative". In order to explain the happenings that we are trying to explain "conservative" hypotheses conflict with some of our previous beliefs, but the fewer the better. The force of conservatism (even in a context of revolution) consists in the capability of inheriting somehow the evidence of the old hypotheses and beliefs.

Good hypotheses are "general", able to accommodate all relevant cases.

The third quality is the quality of "simplicity". When there are hypotheses to choose between, and their claims are equal except in respect of simplicity, we choose the one that looks simple. Generality with simplicity is actually what we want. When our estrangement from the past is excessive, the imagination boggles, and high talent is needed to find one's way about in the new setting.

The fourth quality is "refutability". If hypotheses predict nothing, are confirmed by nothing, they are not good hypotheses. "Refutability" like "conservatism", "generality" and "simplicity" is a matter of degree.

"Modesty" is the fifth quality. Good hypotheses do not explain everything at the same time. They concentrate on precise questions and specific fields neglecting the rest.

Many ways lead to our hypotheses. We inherit most of them in the appropriate fields in which we grow up and are socialized. Those fields keep on evolving. Each one of us participates in the enterprise of adding and dropping hypotheses. Continuity and sizeable disruptions make the changes in our webs of beliefs and hypotheses manageable.

7 Bibliography

Bayne, T., Thought. A Very Short Introduction (Oxford: Oxford University Press, 2013).

Davidson, D., Essays on Actions and Events (Oxford: Clarendon Press, 1989).

Davidson, D., Inquiries into Truth and Interpretation (Oxford: Clarendon Press, 1991).

Davidson, D., Subjective, Intersubjective, Objective (Oxford: Clarendon Press, 2001).

Griffiths, A. P. (Ed.), Knowledge and Belief (Oxford: Oxford University Press, 1968).

Nilsson, N. J., Understanding Beliefs (Cambridge, Massachusetts: The MIT Press, 2014).

Popper, K. R., Conjectures and Refutations. The Growth of Scientific Knowledge (London: Routledge & Kegan Paul Limited, 1962).

Price, H. H., Belief (London: George Allen & Unwin LTD, 1969).

Quine, W. V., Ullian, J. S., The Web of Belief (New York: Random House, 1970).

Ramsey, F. P., The Foundations of Mathematics and Other Logical Essays (Mansfield Centre, CT: Martino Publishing, 2013).

Deciding

On the basis of our beliefs and motivated by our desires and preferences, we act and decide. Actions are not decisions. Sometimes we act after having deliberated for a while and taken a decision on what to do and how to do it. But there may be situations in which our concrete actions can be taken to be our decisions. In such cases it does not make sense to distinguish sharply between actions and decisions.

When we deliberate before acting or deciding we become sensitive to the requirements that make up the practical environment in which we have to act. Those requirements as practical "oughts" are the reasons that may guide us when acting and deciding and justify our actions and decisions.

My approach is not a Bayesian one simply because I think that probabilistic analyses remain at too great a distance from the factual practice of deciding to be really informative about that practice.

1 Practical Oughts

Ought-sentences in English express on the one hand a prescription and, on the other, a prediction. Only the context will show which is meant. Normally, "If one is tired, one ought to take a rest" would be an example of the subjunctive-governing use to express a prescriptive recommendation and "If one takes a rest, one ought to wake refreshed" of the indicative-governing use expressing a justified prediction. The indicative use works for any verb, but the subjunctive usually works only for task-verbs. Advices, preferences and prescriptions are linked to the subjunctive use; predictions to the indicative. The reasons appropriate to the subjunctive are preferential, those to the indicative are evidential (White, 139ff.).

John Broome, less concerned with the grammatical use, distinguishes normative and non-normative oughts, owned and unowned oughts, qualified and unqualified oughts, and objective and prospective oughts.

Normative oughts prescribe or recommend something, for instance: "You ought to look both ways before crossing the road". Non-normative oughts predict something or express an expectation as in "These raspberries ought to ripen in June". "Ownership" as a criterion to distinguish sorts of ought indicates agent-relativity. Not owned oughts do not mention anybody, so the sentence "Life ought not to be so unfair".

Oughts may be qualified as moral, rational or prudential oughts. The all-things-considered ought is the ought John Broome calls "central ought", an unqualified ought. In the central ought come different components together. The "central ought", important in Broome's project of defining reasons in terms of "ought", is characterized as "normative", "owned", "unqualified" and "prospective".

"Objective oughts" are outcome oughts. There are situations where you ought to do what will have the best consequences. "Prospective oughts" present a portfolio of possible outcomes, each associated with a probability. Outcome oughts tell us what we ought objectively to do. Prospective oughts are relative to probabilities and expected values.

John Broome adds to his classification of the meanings of ought a further classification: the classification of different "requirements". Broome distinguishes "property" requirements, "sources" requirements, and "needs" requirements. "Property" requirements appear in sentences like "Staying healthy requires hard work" or "Writing scientific papers requires determination". "Sources" requirements denote persons or things that have some sort of authority and are the requirement's source ("The law requires x" or "The bill requires payment"). "Needs" requirements appear in sentences like "Trees require water" or "The patient requires constant attention". Broome calls the requirements that necessarily contribute to determine what we ought to do "normative" requirements. After a long and complex argument Broome arrives at the conclusion that "ought" behaves like normative requirement (Broome, 127).

John Broome's subtle distinctions and classifications show that there are different kinds of practical oughts that become relevant in decision situations, that is, in all those situations in which we have to decide reacting appropriately to many and heterogeneous factors, conditions and requirements.

2 Deliberate Decisions

In the third book of his "Nicomachean Ethics" Aristotle treats choice as something related to the means we need to obtain what we wish and to the things that are in our own power. Aristotle conceives of the object of choice as the "the result of previous deliberation". No one chooses things that are not in his power, but only the things that he thinks could be brought about by his own efforts. And while wish relates rather to the end, choice relates to the means. Aristotle's main example is health-related. We wish to be healthy as an end, but we choose the acts which will make us healthy, and we wish to be happy and say we do, but we cannot well say we choose to be so, as being happy does not seem to be in our own power.

Deliberation is for Aristotle not about everything. About eternal things no sensible man deliberates, e.g. about the material universe or the incommensurability of the diagonal and the side of a square. No one deliberates either about the things that involve movement always happening in the same way (e.g. the solstices and the risings of the stars), nor about things that happen now in one way, now in another (e.g. droughts and rains), nor about chance events. For none of these things can be brought about by our own efforts. For Aristotle, we deliberate about things that are in our power and can be done. And we always deliberate about means, not about ends.

Deliberation like choice is about means, and about what is in our power. Aristotle interprets choice as deliberate choice or "deliberate desire of things in our power". In his own words: "The object of choice being one of the things in our power which is desired after deliberation, choice will be deliberate desire of things in our own power; for when we have decided as a result of deliberation, we desire in accordance with our deliberation" (Aristotle, 58).

3 Decisions without Previous Deliberations

Not every decision is preceded by deliberation. In many cases we decide without deliberating previously, and most of the time our actions are our actual decisions.

Mind has a place in nature. Deciding and acting individuals are not "intelligible" beings, citizens of an ideal world, but empirical, physical agents capable of reacting appropriately in natural environments, shaping and transforming them according to their own plans and intentions. When we describe their functioning, we use sometimes physical and sometimes psychological vocabulary, both vocabularies being sufficiently justified.

Our conceptual descriptions help us understand aspects, traits and features of complex phenomena. They do not refer, however, to separate inner entities that could be atomistically grasped and then aggregated according to some compositionality principle. Creating inner entities cannot be the task of philosophical reasoning. Philosophizing, we try to understand and explain the world, human beings, and how world and human beings interact. It would not be appropriate to expect reality to adapt to our conceptual or terminological distinctions, delivering the entities we may have assumed in some of our explanatory enterprises.

4 Letting Things Happen

When we act, intentionally or with a specific intention, we cause things to happen. For the results or outcomes of our actions there are, therefore, causal explanations that cite our actions and interventions as the causal agents. Causal explanations furnish relevant information about what happened. When we are the causal agents, the information provided by causal explanations mentions us as the relevant causal factors. Such explanations may be counter-factual, providing a pattern of counterfactual dependence of a special sort: "Had x not intervened, had x not acted, the state or event to be explained would not have come about". What really counts causally is then presented counterfactually.

We can make things happen, acting intentionally. And we can let easily predictable things happen, abstaining from acting or intervening, that is, omitting to act. There are different varieties of omission. Sometimes when we do not do something, it would be entirely unreasonable to be blamed for it. Due to our complete ignorance of what happened, we had no opportunity to intervene, and this ignorance is not the result of negligence. At the other extreme of blameworthiness, there are culpable omissions describable as positive acts of abstaining from intervention. In some cases it may be difficult to draw the line between acts and omissions. Between the extremes there are various kinds of omission, some of them are the result of negligent ignorance, others are conscious omissions as the result of laziness rather than some discreditable motive.

Similarly, there are active decisions as causal interventions and many kinds of not positively deciding which could be interpreted somehow as cases of intentionally abstaining from deciding.

5 Bibliography

Aristotle, Nicomachean Ethics (London: Oxford University Press, 1966).

Broome, J., Rationality Through Reasoning (Oxford: Wiley Blackwell, 2013).

Glover, J., Causing Death and Saving Lives (London: Penguin Books, 1990).

White, A. R., Modal Thinking (Oxford: Basil Blackwell, 1975).

Woodward, J., Making Things Happen. A Theory of Causal Explanation (Oxford: Oxford University Press, 2003).

Bandaufstellung

Alle erschienenen Bücher können unter der angegebenen
ISBN direkt online (http://www.logos-verlag.de) oder
per Fax (030 - 42 85 10 92) beim Logos Verlag Berlin
bestellt werden.